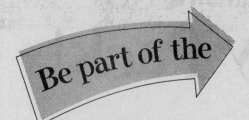

Dalmatian 🐾 Press
Puppy Pack!™

Your pictures and ideas could be **spotted**

D1312152

✂ CUT ALONG DOTTED LINES

Dear Dalmatian Press,

_____

_____

_____

_____

_____

_____

Your Friend, _____

WRITE YOUR NAME HERE   WRITE YOUR AGE

_____   _____

WHERE DID YOU BUY THIS BOOK?   **PHONE NUMBER:** (In case your letter or picture is picked!)

12803 JURASSIC GIANTS

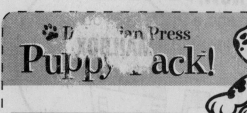

🐾 Dalmatian Press
Puppy Pack!

YOUR NAME _____

I wrote to Dalmatian Press on: _____
and now I am a member of the DPPP.   DATE

✂ CUT ALONG DOTTED LINE AND **KEEP FOR YOURSELF!**

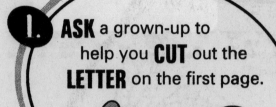

Here is how to join the

Dalmatian 🐾 Press
Puppy Pack!™

1. **ASK** a grown-up to help you **CUT** out the **LETTER** on the first page.

2. **WRITE** and **TELL** us what you...
- like about our coloring books.
- want us to make a coloring book about.
- would change about our books.

3. **ASK** a grown-up for an **ENVELOPE** and a **STAMP.** Be sure to fill out the envelope like **THIS:**

> STAMP
>
> Your name and address
>
> Dalmatian Press
> P.O. Box 682068
> Franklin, TN 37068-2068

4. **NOW,** put your letter and a **PICTURE** you have colored in a **MAILBOX.**

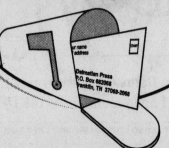

5. **WHO** knows? Maybe your **PICTURE** and **IDEAS** will be spotted on the next **DALMATIAN** Press book!

How many words can you make using the letters in:

DINOSAUR

_____

_____

_____

_____

_____

_____

_____

_____

WHICH ONE IS DIFFERENT?

How many words can you make using the letters in:

UNDERWATER

_____

_____

_____

_____

_____

_____

_____

_____

_____

SHADOW MATCHING

USE THE GRID
TO DRAW THE
DINOSAUR

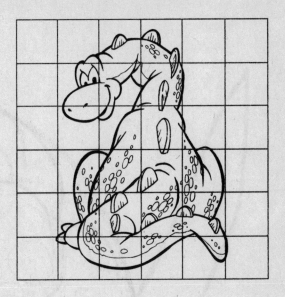

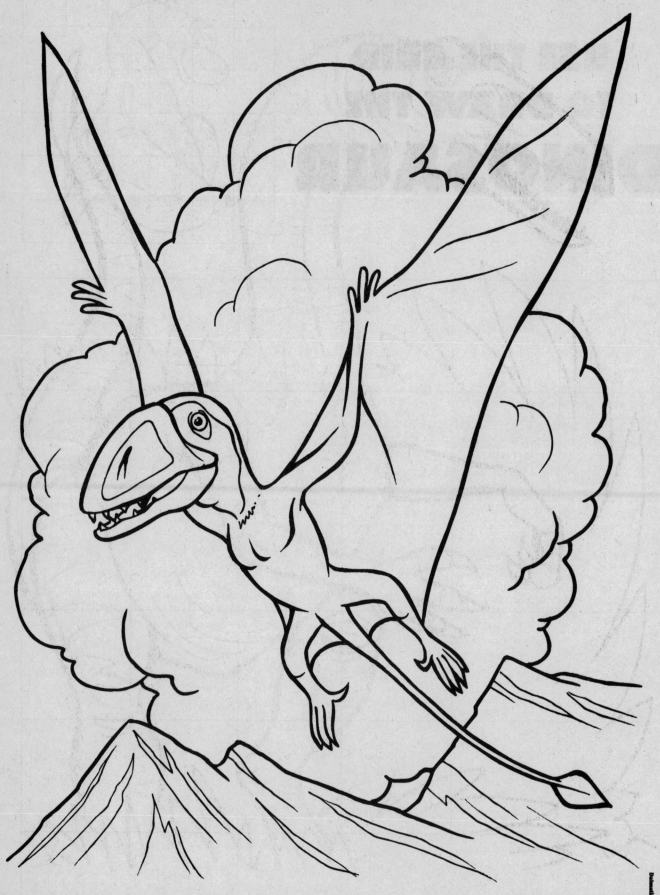

WHICH ONE IS DIFFERENT?

DOT-TO-DOT

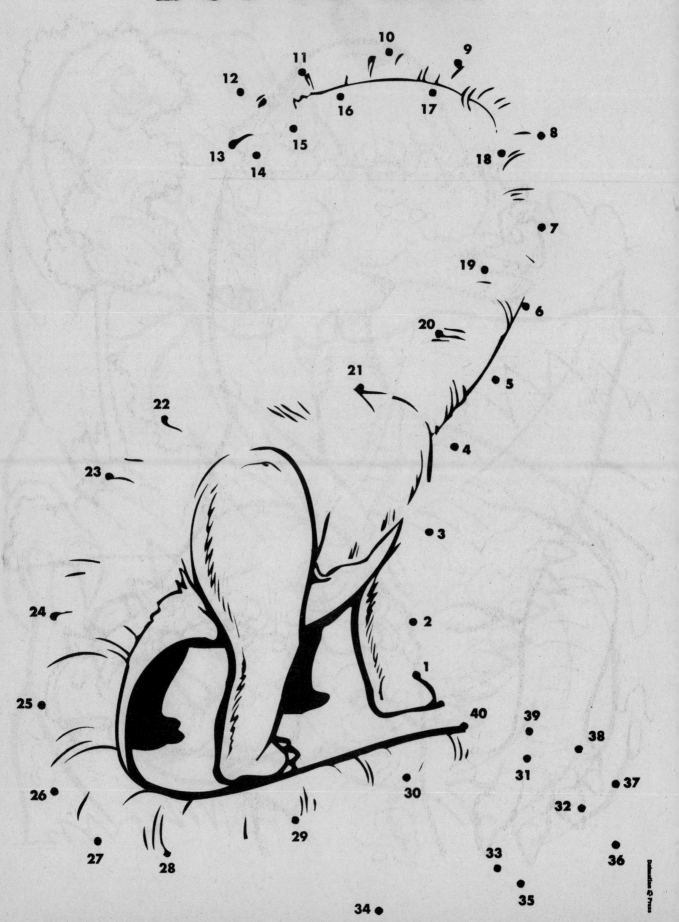

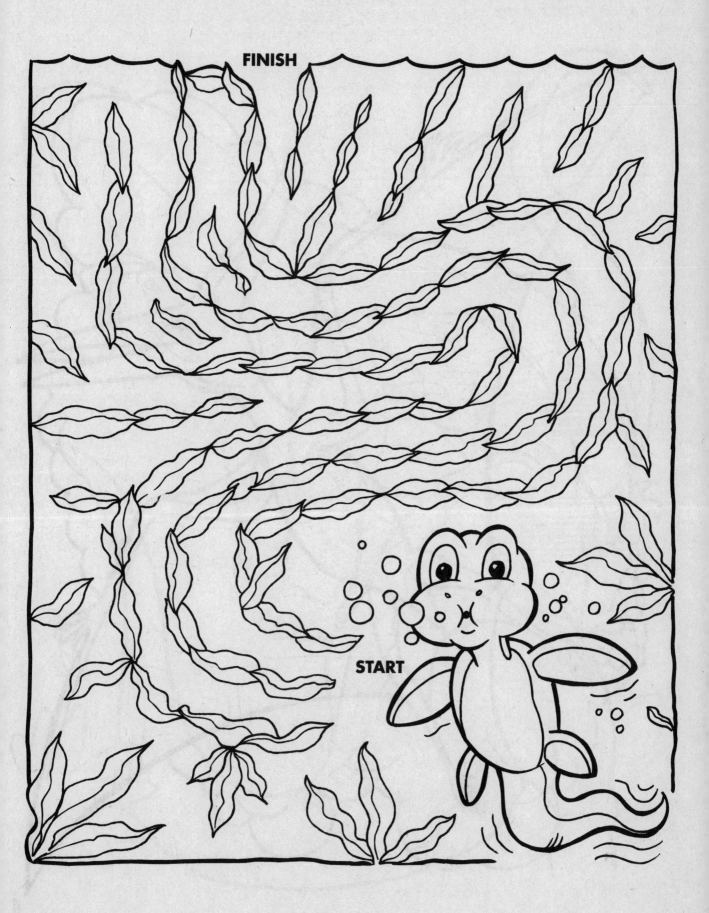

How many words can you make using the letters in:

PTERODACTYL

_____

_____

_____

_____

_____

_____

_____

_____

_____

WHICH ONE IS DIFFERENT?

DOT-TO-DOT

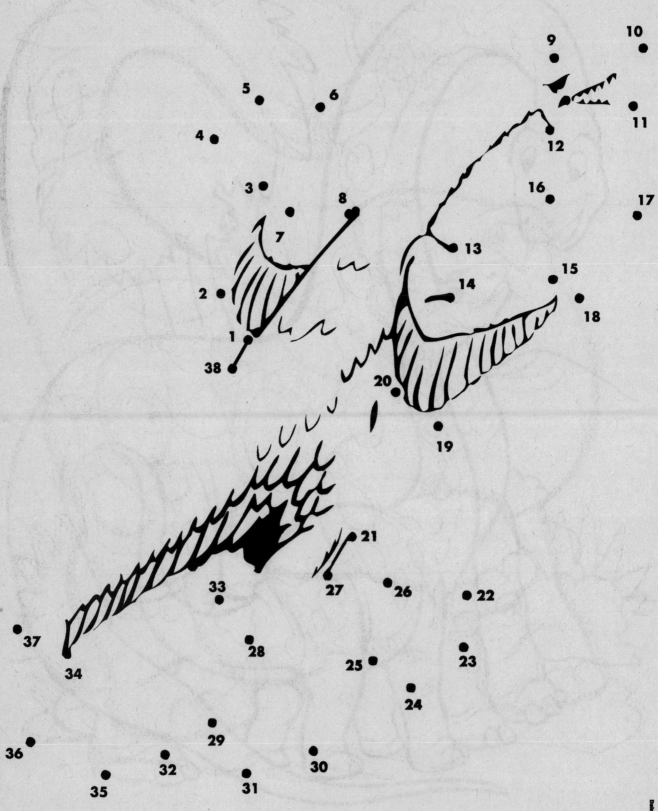

Dalmatian Press

START

FINISH

USE THE GRID
TO DRAW THE
DINOSAUR

DOT-TO-DOT

WHICH ONE IS DIFFERENT?

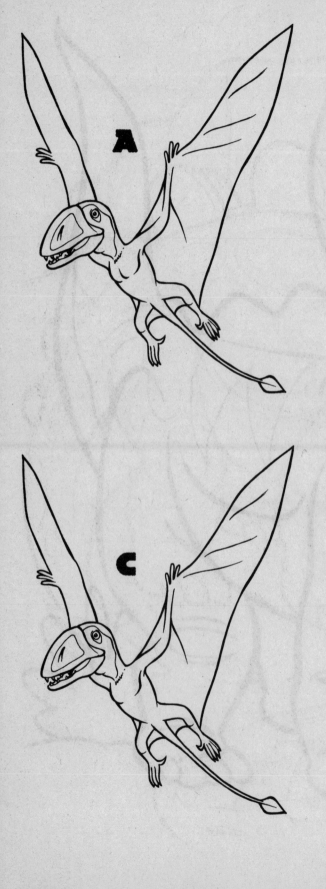

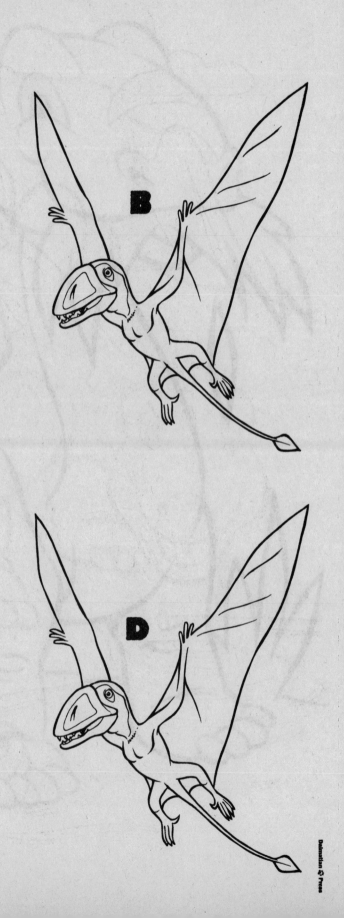

Dalmatian Press

SHADOW MATCHING

DOT-TO-DOT

USE THE GRID
TO DRAW THE
DINOSAUR

DOT-TO-DOT

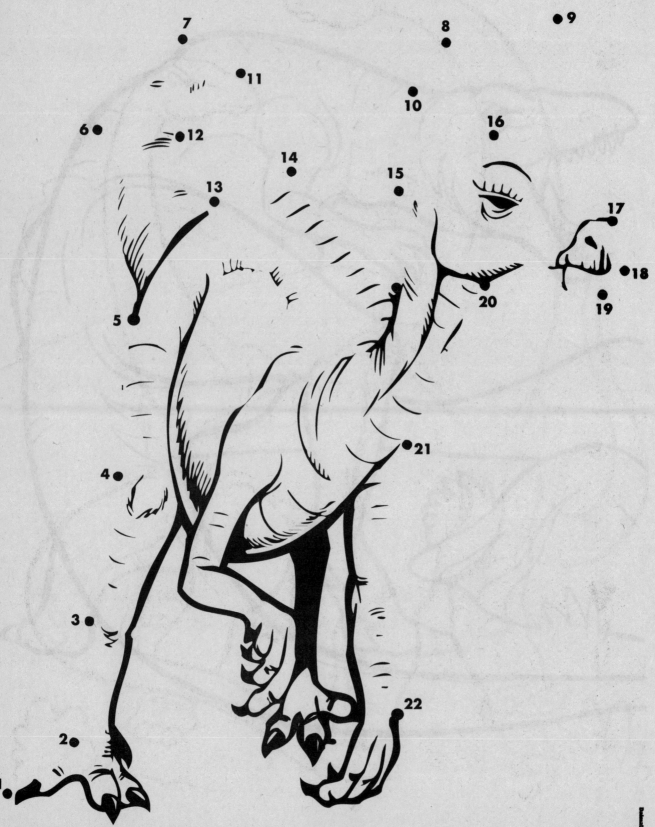

WHICH ONE IS DIFFERENT?

DOT-TO-DOT

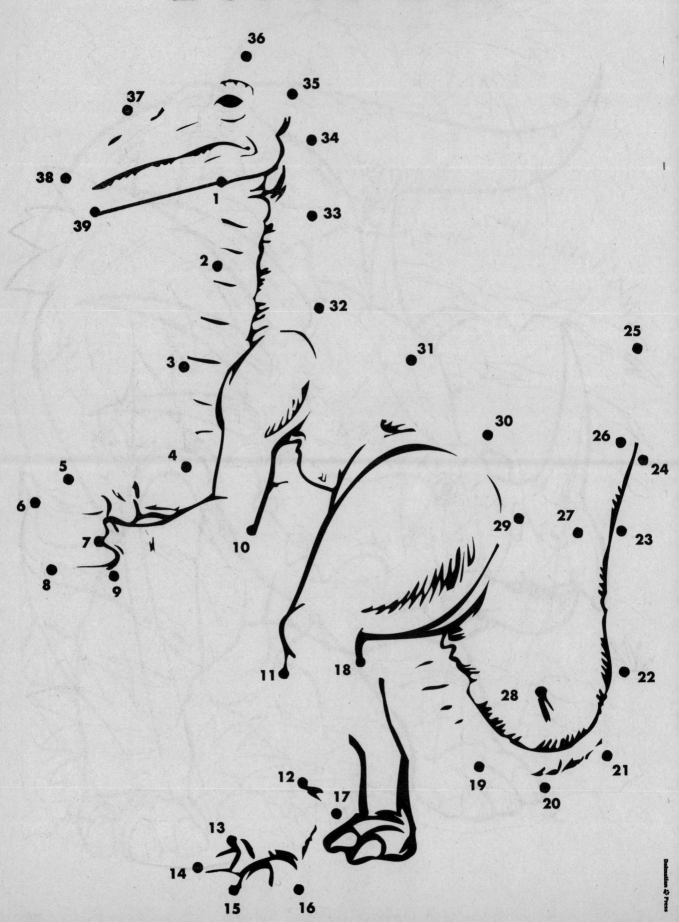

How many words can you make using the letters in:

EXTINCTION

_____

_____

_____

_____

_____

_____

_____

_____

USE THE GRID
TO DRAW THE
DINOSAUR

WHICH ONE IS DIFFERENT?

SHADOW MATCHING

SHADOW MATCHING

USE THE GRID TO DRAW THE DINOSAUR

How many words can you make using the letters in:

JIANGJUNMIAOSAURUS

_____

_____

_____

_____

_____

_____

_____

_____

_____

Jiangjunmiaosaurus

WHICH ONE IS DIFFERENT?

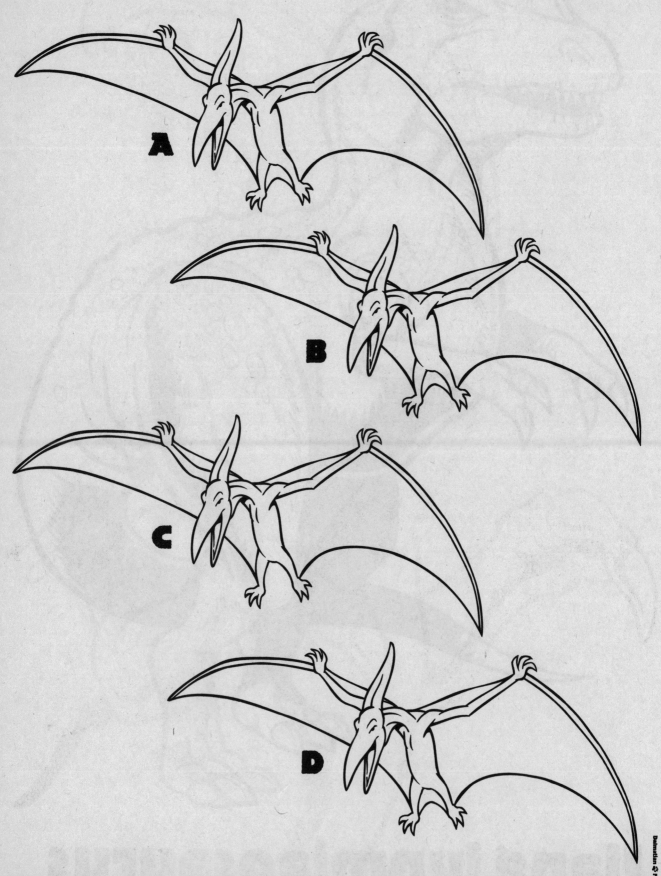

Dalmatian Press

DOT-TO-DOT

START

FINISH

DOT-TO-DOT

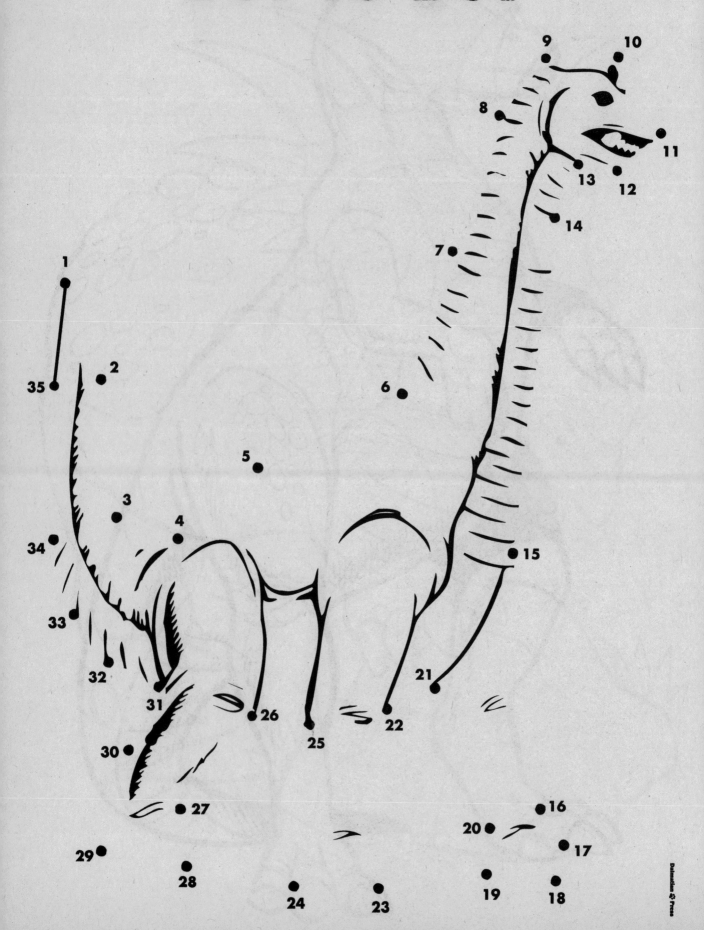

USE THE GRID
TO DRAW THE
DINOSAUR

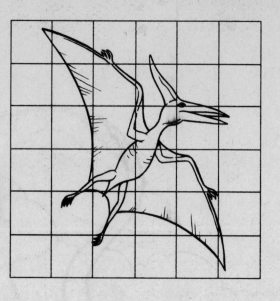

SHADOW MATCHING

WHICH ONE IS DIFFERENT?

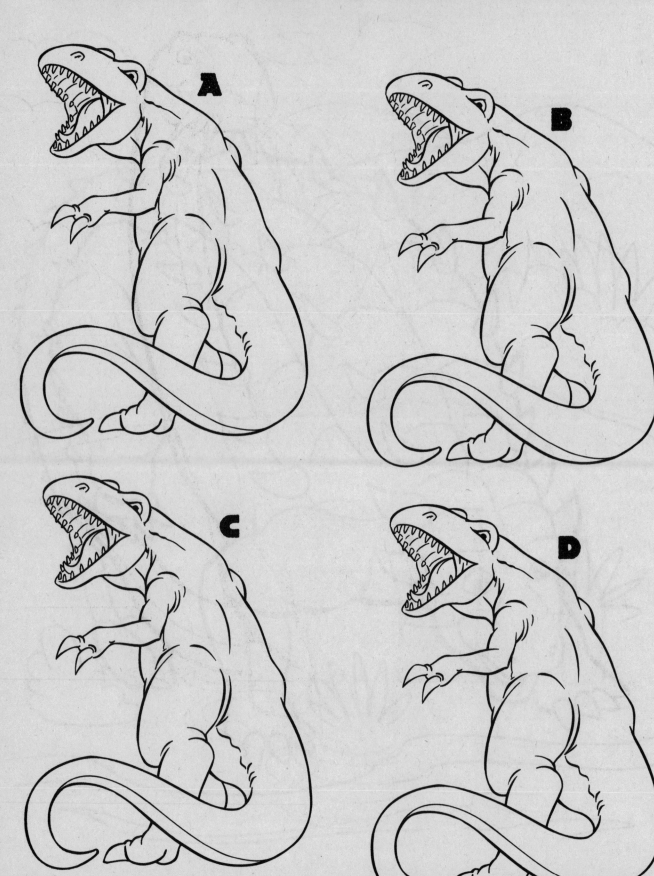

A

B

C

D

START

FINISH

How many words can you make using the letters in:

FEROCIOUS

_____

_____

_____

_____

_____

_____

_____

_____

_____

USE THE GRID
TO DRAW THE
DINOSAUR

WHICH ONE IS DIFFERENT?

A

B

C

D

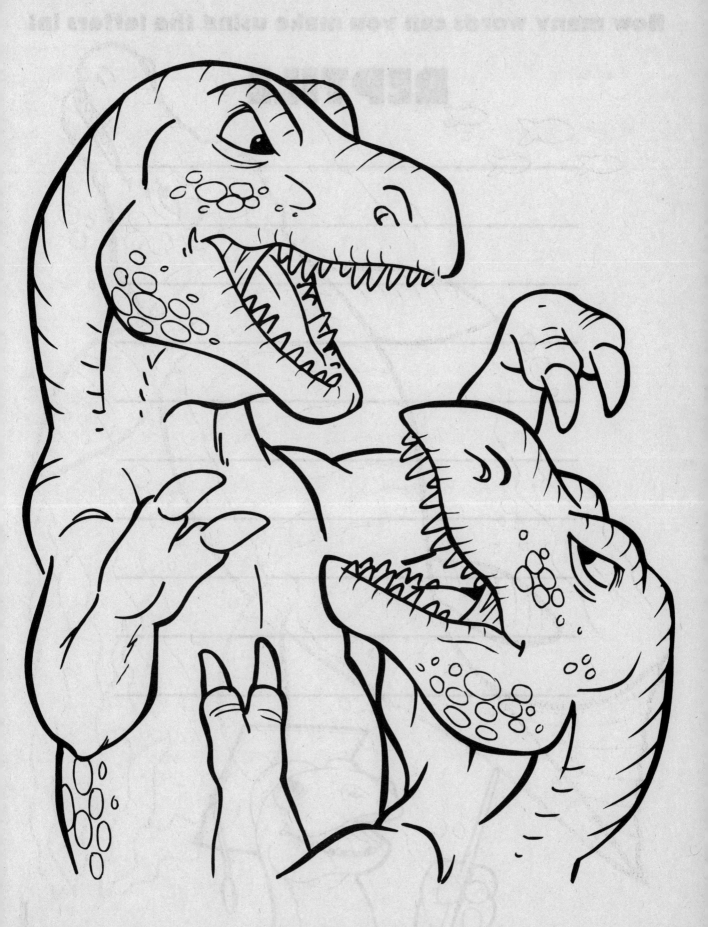

How many words can you make using the letters in:

REPTILE

_____

_____

_____

_____

_____

_____

_____

_____

_____

USE THE GRID
TO DRAW THE
DINOSAUR

How many words can you make using the letters in:

LEAELLYNASAURA

_____

_____

_____

_____

_____

_____

_____

_____

_____

Dalmatian © Press

Leaellynasaura

SHADOW MATCHING

WHICH ONE IS DIFFERENT?

A

B

C

D

START

FINISH

DOT-TO-DOT

USE THE GRID
TO DRAW THE
DINOSAUR

DOT-TO-DOT

How many words can you make using the letters in:

SABER TOOTH

_____

_____

_____

_____

_____

_____

_____

_____

_____

WHICH ONE IS DIFFERENT?

A

B

C

D

Dalmatian Press

USE THE GRID
TO DRAW THE
DINOSAUR

Tyrannosaurus Rex

How many words can you make using the letters in:

DIPLODOCUS

_____

_____

_____

_____

_____

_____

_____

_____

WHICH ONE IS DIFFERENT?

A

B

C

D

Dalmatian Press

Dalmatian Press

USE THE GRID TO DRAW THE DINOSAUR

Ultrasaurus

How many words can you make using the letters in:

ULTRASAURUS

_____

_____

_____

_____

_____

_____

_____

_____

SHADOW MATCHING

WHICH ONE IS DIFFERENT?

How many words can you make using the letters in:

OURANOSAURUS

_____

_____

_____

_____

_____

_____

_____

_____

_____

Ouranosaurus

DOT-TO-DOT

USE THE GRID
TO DRAW THE
DINOSAUR

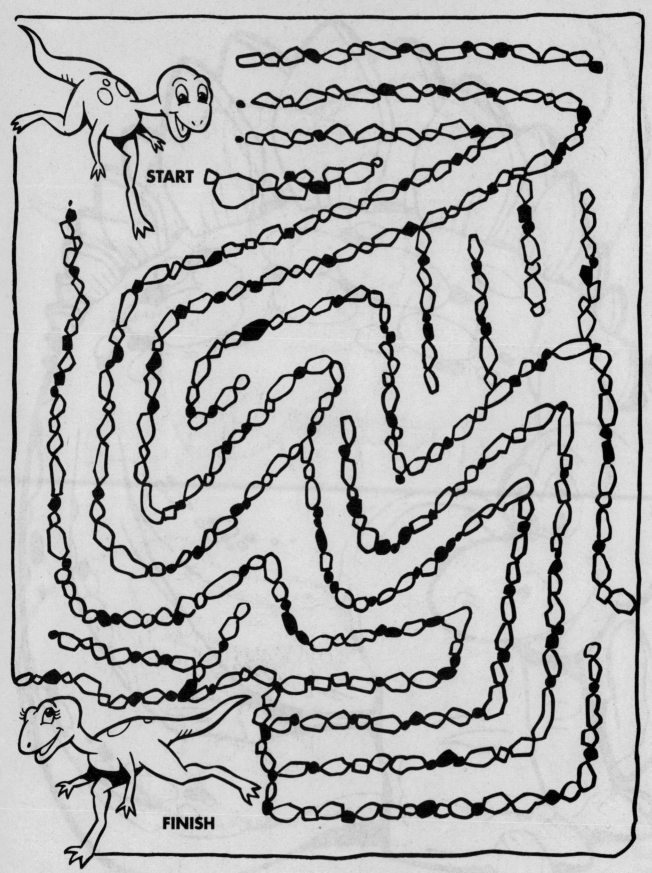

START

FINISH

WHICH ONE IS DIFFERENT?

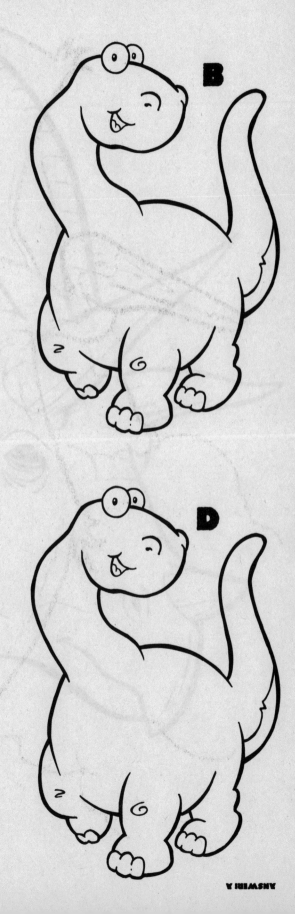

DOT-TO-DOT

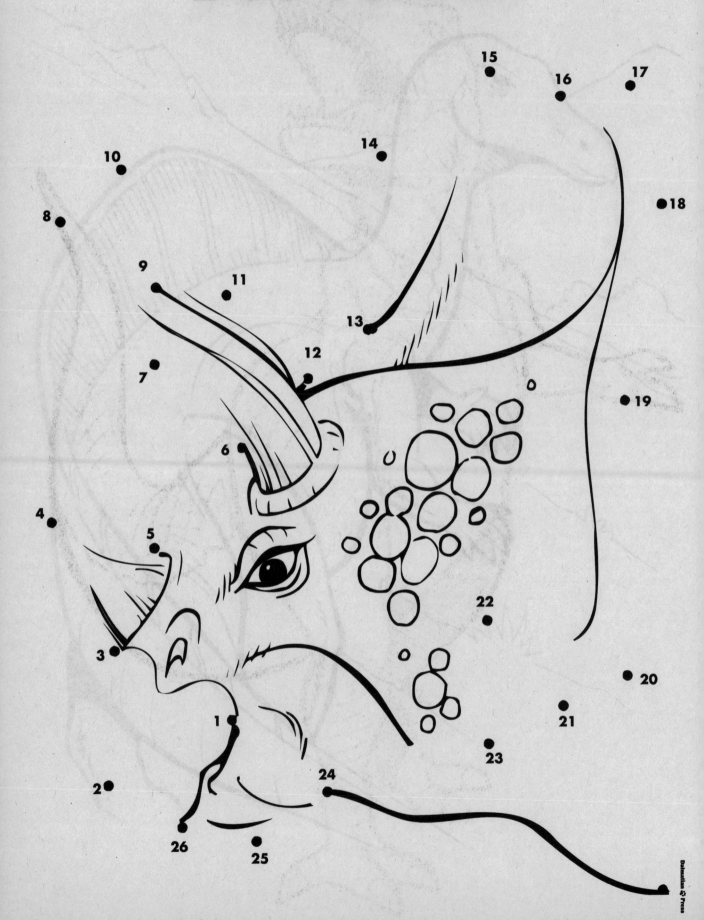

SHADOW MATCHING

START

FINISH

USE THE GRID
TO DRAW THE
DINOSAUR

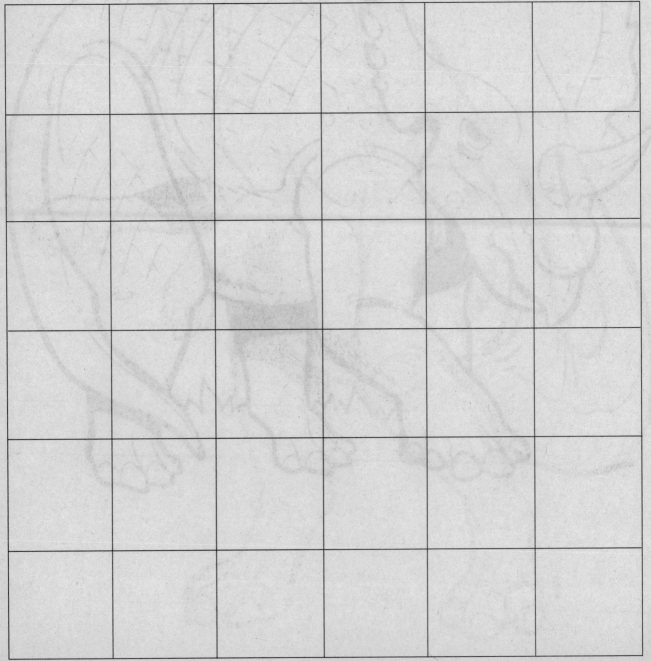

Dalmatian Press

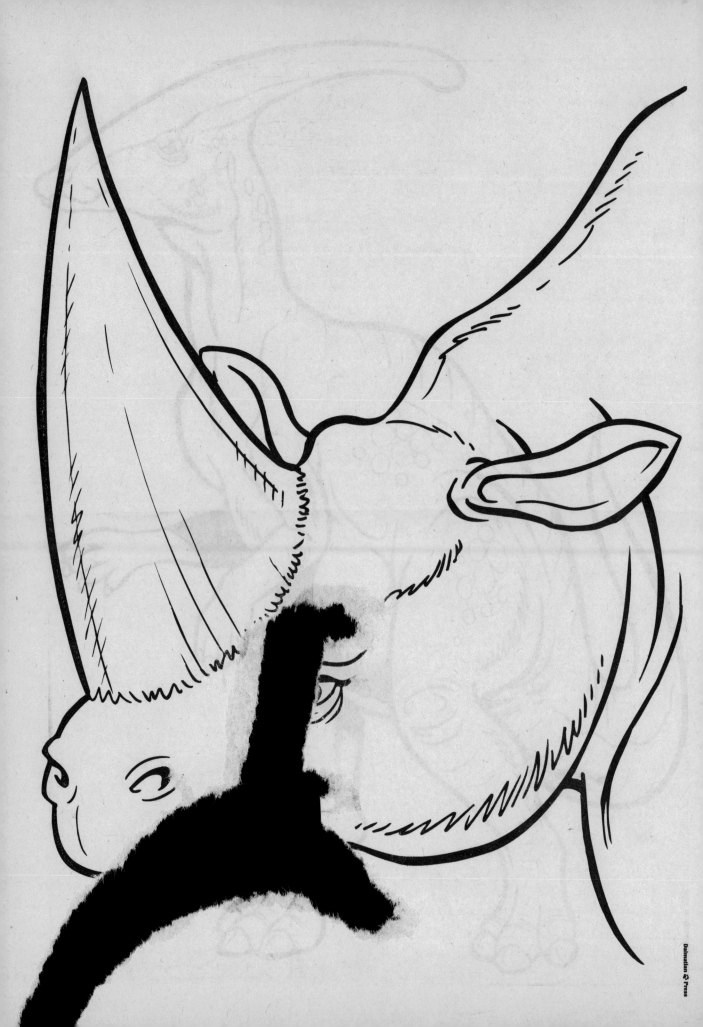

DOT-TO-DOT

WHICH ONE IS DIFFERENT?

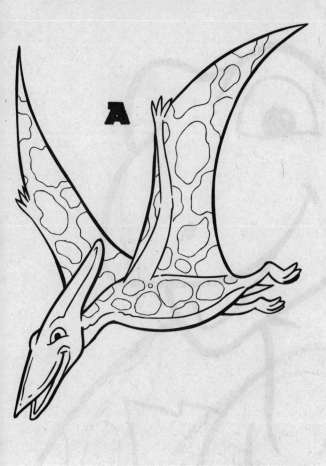

A

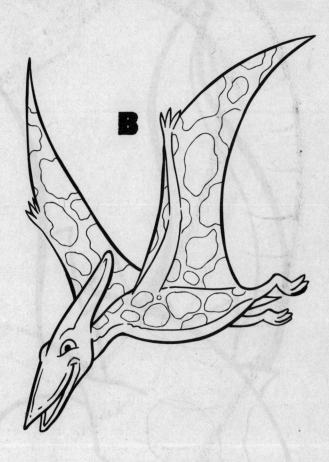

B

C

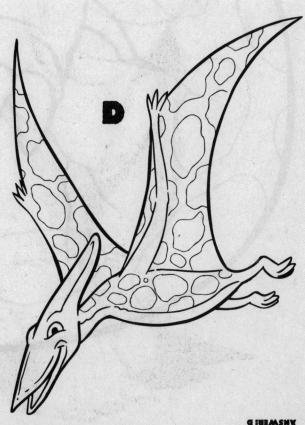

D

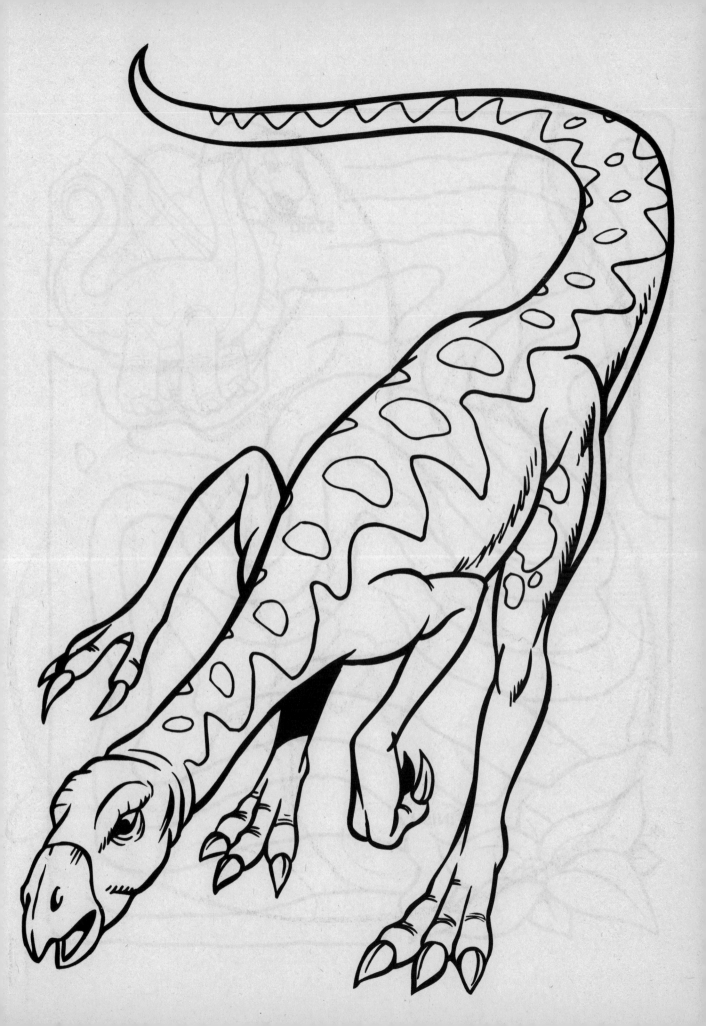

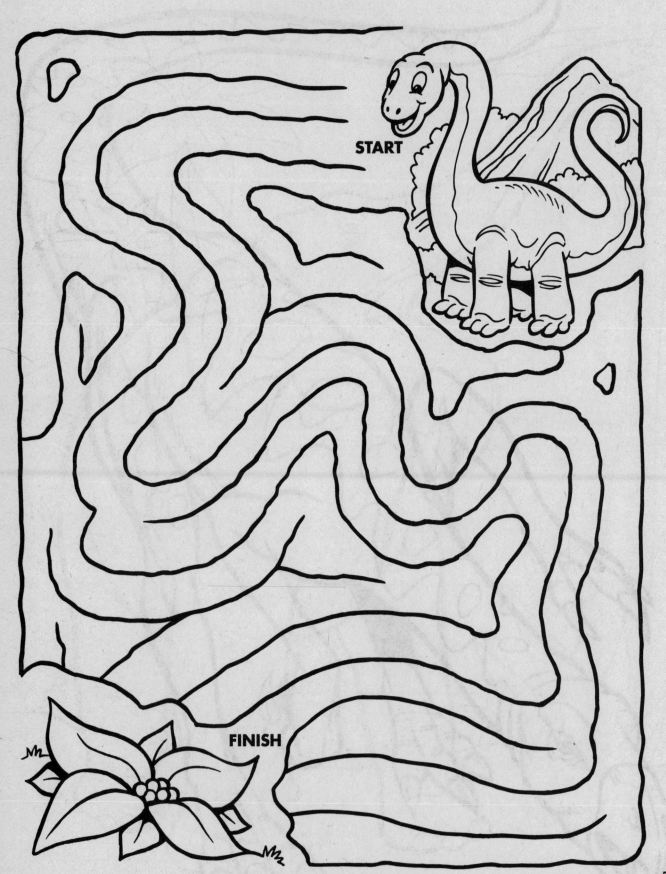

START

FINISH

DOT-TO-DOT

USE THE GRID TO DRAW THE DINOSAUR

SHADOW MATCHES
USE THE GRID
TO DRAW THE
DINOSAUR

SHADOW MATCHING

How many words can you make using the letters in:

PALEONTOLOGIST

_____

_____

_____

_____

_____

_____

_____

_____

WHICH ONE IS DIFFERENT?

START

FINISH

USE THE GRID TO DRAW THE DINOSAUR

How many words can you make using the letters in:

PACHYCEPHALOSAURUS

_____

_____

_____

_____

_____

_____

_____

_____

_____

Pachycephalosaurus

DOT-TO-DOT

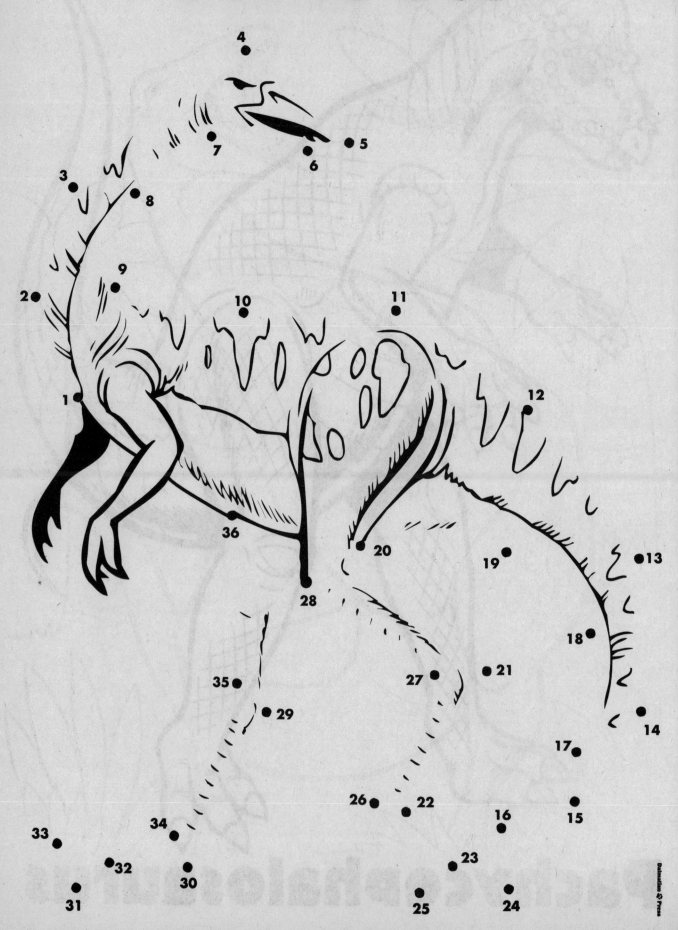

WHICH ONE IS DIFFERENT?

DOT-TO-DOT

USE THE GRID
TO DRAW THE
DINOSAUR

SHADOW MATCHING

WHICH ONE IS DIFFERENT?

Dalmatian Press

How many words can you make using the letters in:

WOOLLY MAMMOTH

_____

_____

_____

_____

_____

_____

_____

_____

_____

DOT-TO-DOT

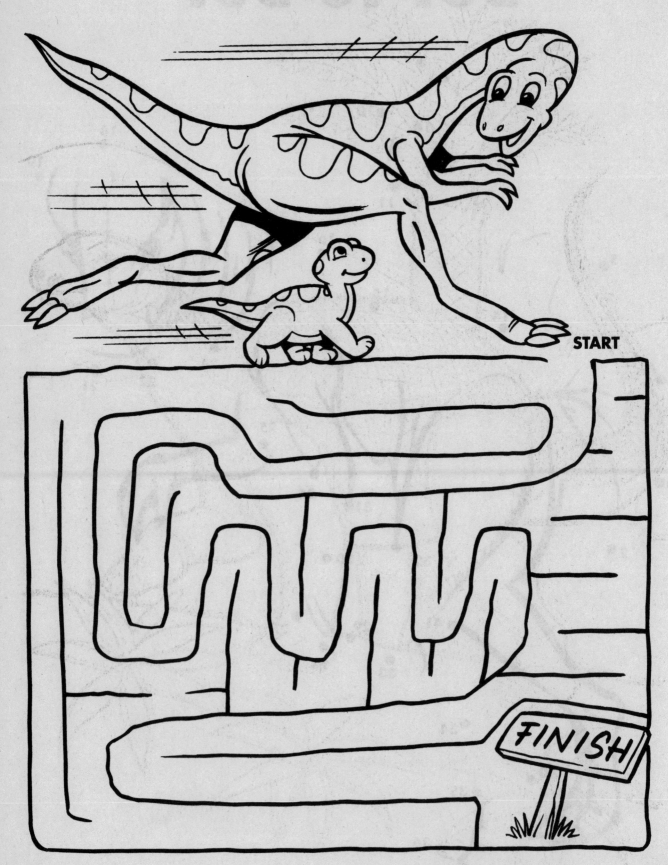

START

FINISH

USE THE GRID
TO DRAW THE
DINOSAUR

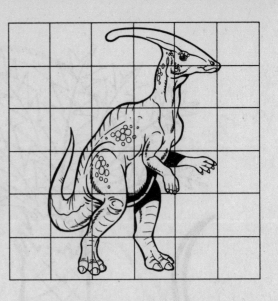

WHICH ONE IS DIFFERENT?

A

B

C

D

How many words can you make using the letters in:

TRICERATOPS

_____

_____

_____

_____

_____

_____

_____

_____

_____

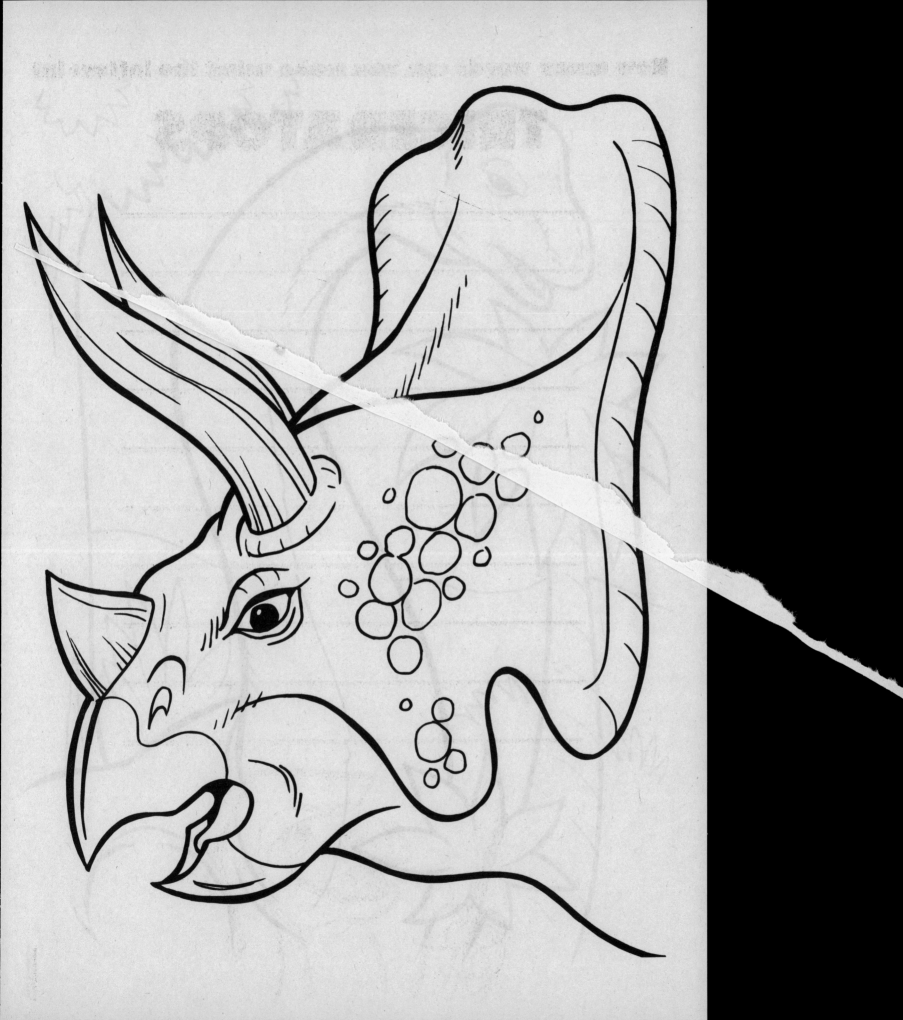

USE THE GRID TO DRAW THE DINOSAUR

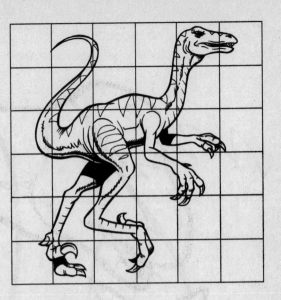

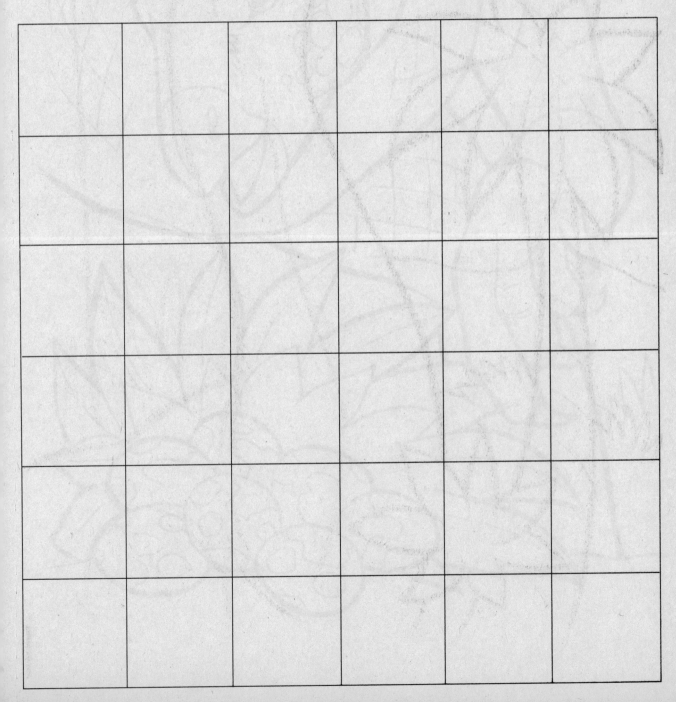

WHICH ONE IS DIFFERENT?

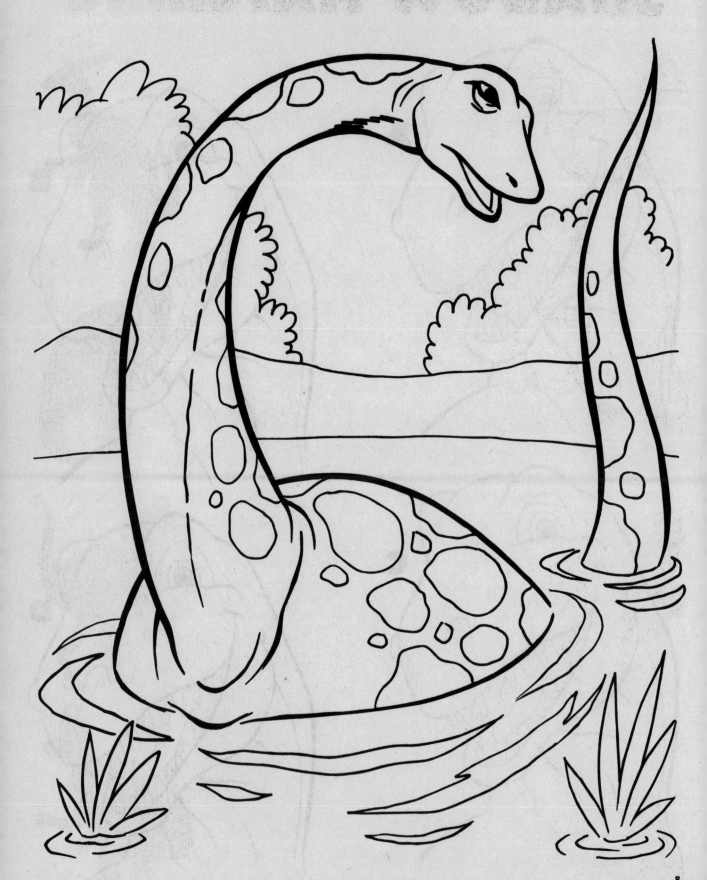

SHADOW MATCHING

START

FINISH

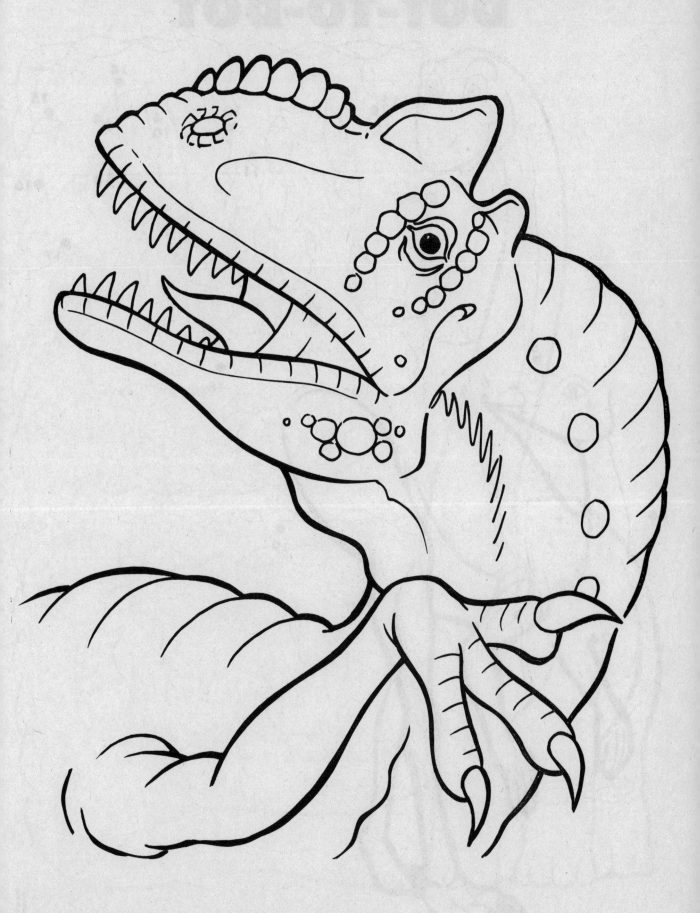

DOT-TO-DOT

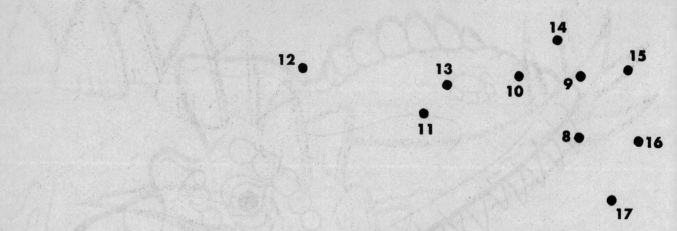

How many words can you make using the letters in:

EUOPLOCEPHALUS

_____

_____

_____

_____

_____

_____

_____

_____

_____

Euoplocephalus

USE THE GRID
TO DRAW THE
DINOSAUR

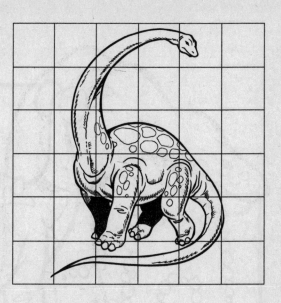

DOT-TO-DOT

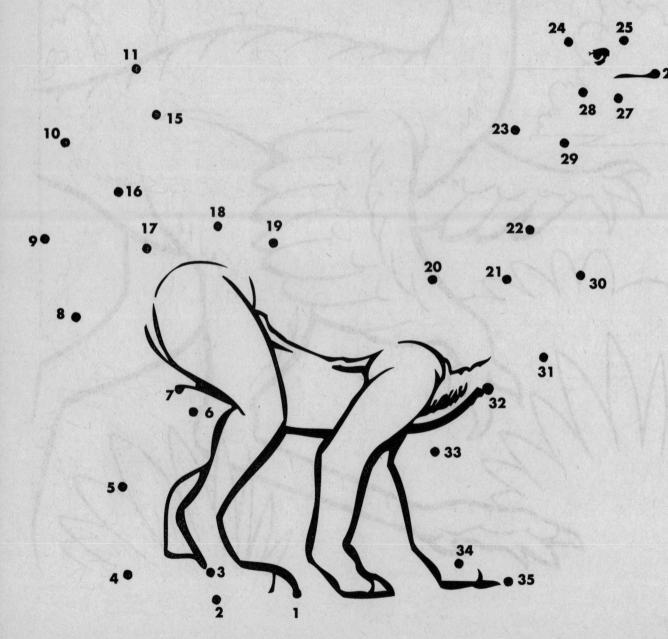

START

FINISH

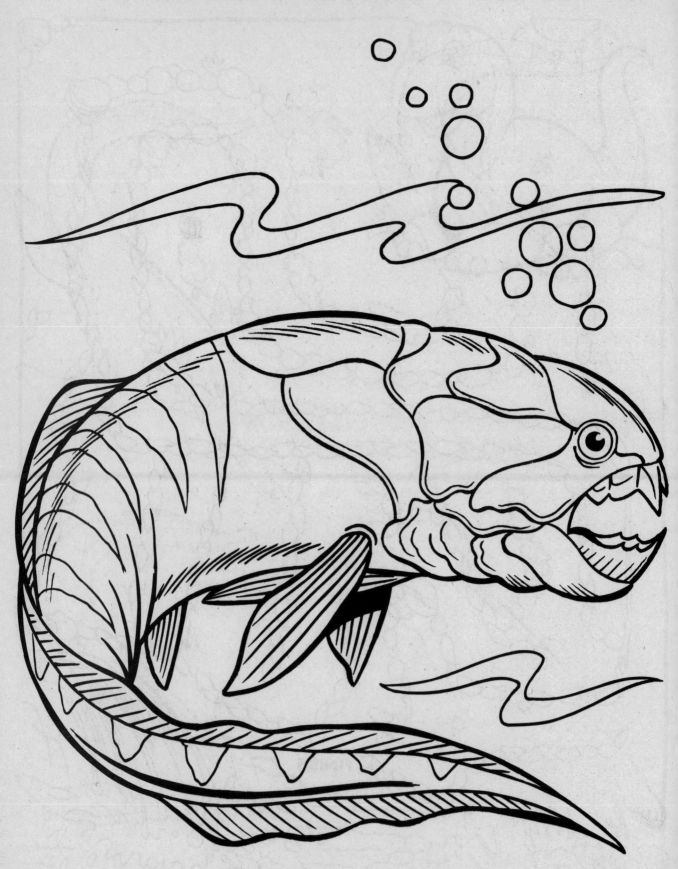

WHICH ONE IS DIFFERENT?

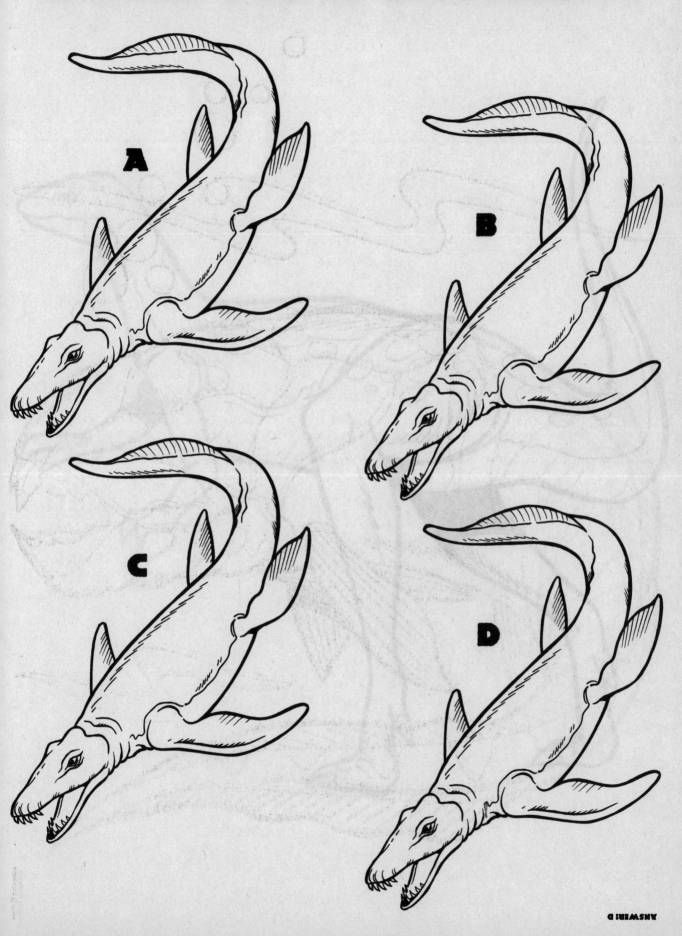

USE THE GRID
TO DRAW THE
DINOSAUR

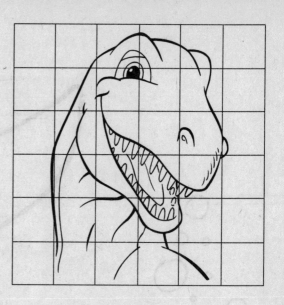

How many words can you make using the letters in:

GIGANTIC

_____

_____

_____

_____

_____

_____

_____

_____

_____

SHADOW MATCHING

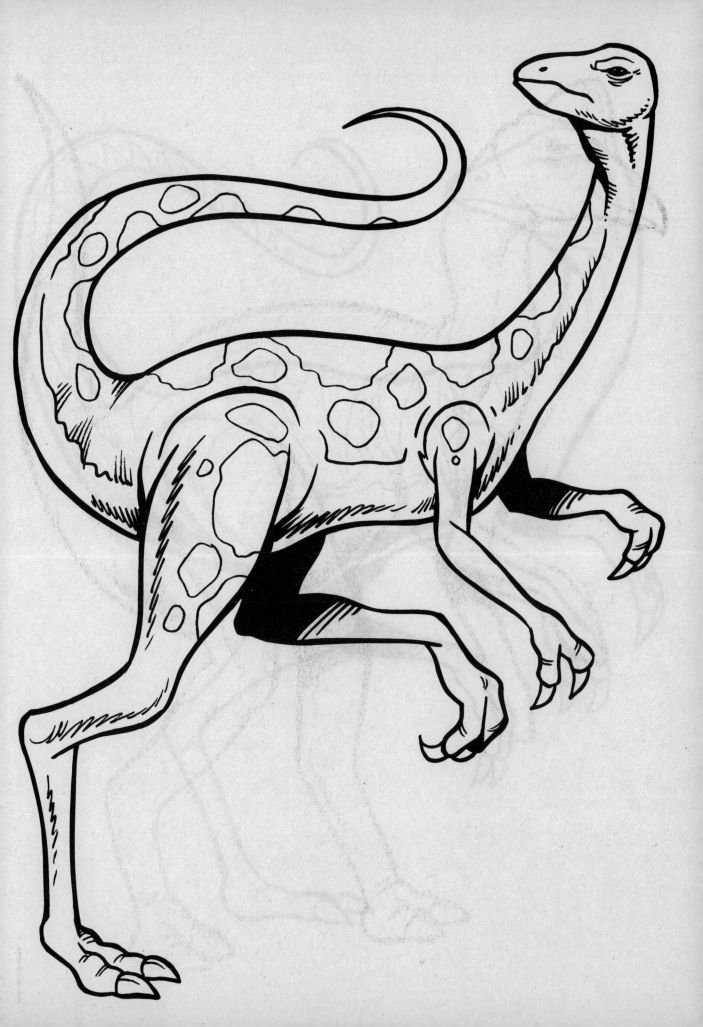

WHICH ONE IS DIFFERENT?

How many words can you make using the letters in:

PREHISTORIC

_____

_____

_____

_____

_____

_____

_____

_____

USE THE GRID TO DRAW THE DINOSAUR

Dalmatian ❀ Press

START

FINISH

WHICH ONE IS DIFFERENT?

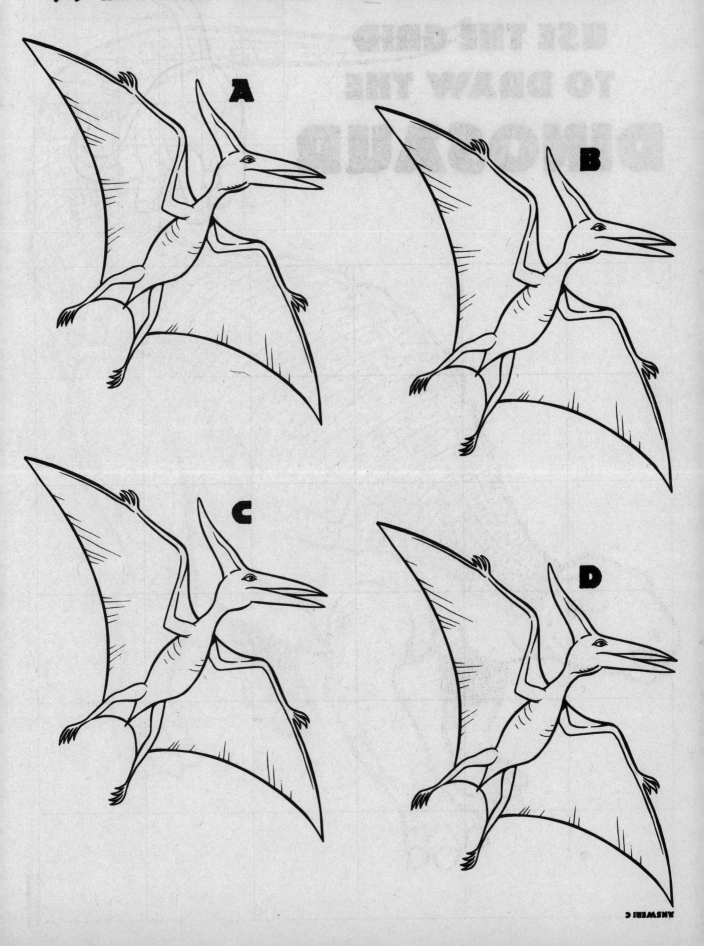

A

B

C

D

USE THE GRID
TO DRAW THE
DINOSAUR

How many words can you make using the letters in:

HUMONGOUS

_____

_____

_____

_____

_____

_____

_____

_____

_____

SHADOW MATCHING

How many words can you make using the letters in:

STEGOSAURUS

_____

_____

_____

_____

_____

_____

_____

_____

_____

DOT-TO-DOT

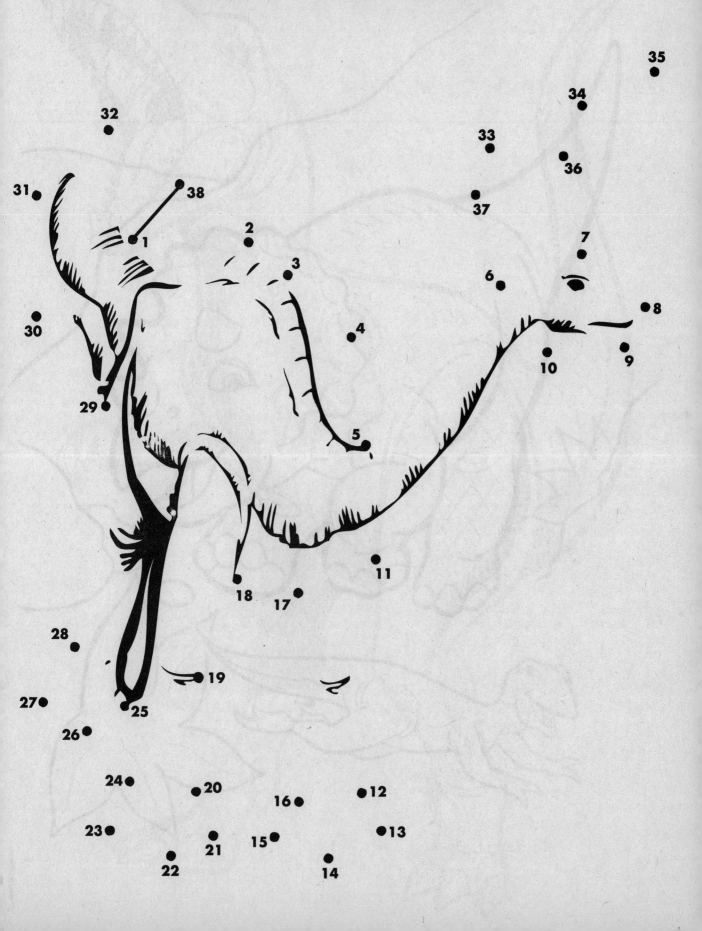

USE THE GRID TO DRAW THE DINOSAUR

START

FINISH

WHICH ONE IS DIFFERENT?

DOT-TO-DOT

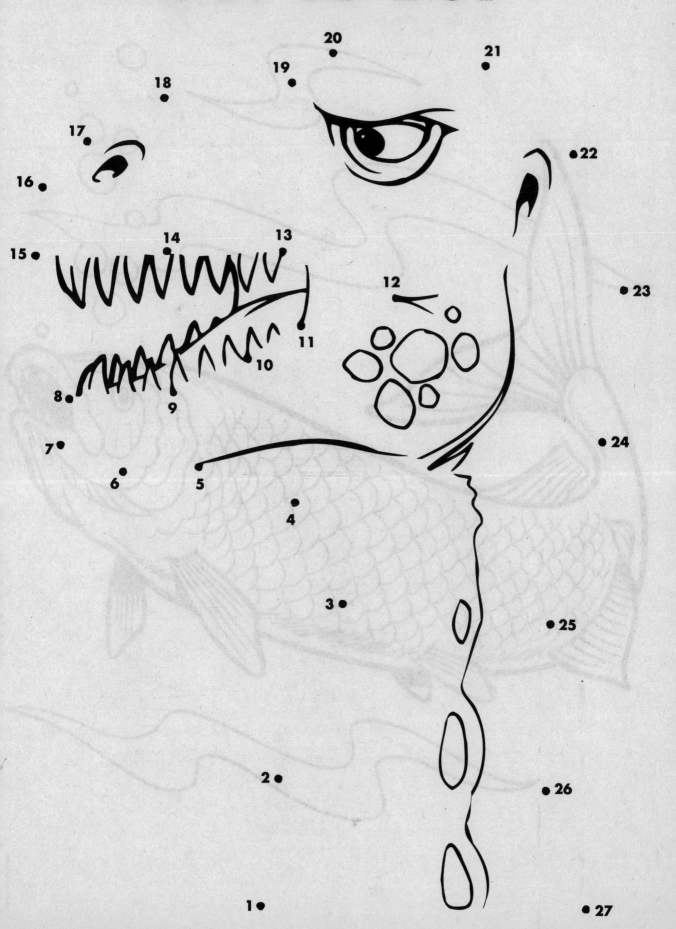

How many words can you make using the letters in:

VELOCIRAPTOR

_____

_____

_____

_____

_____

_____

_____

_____

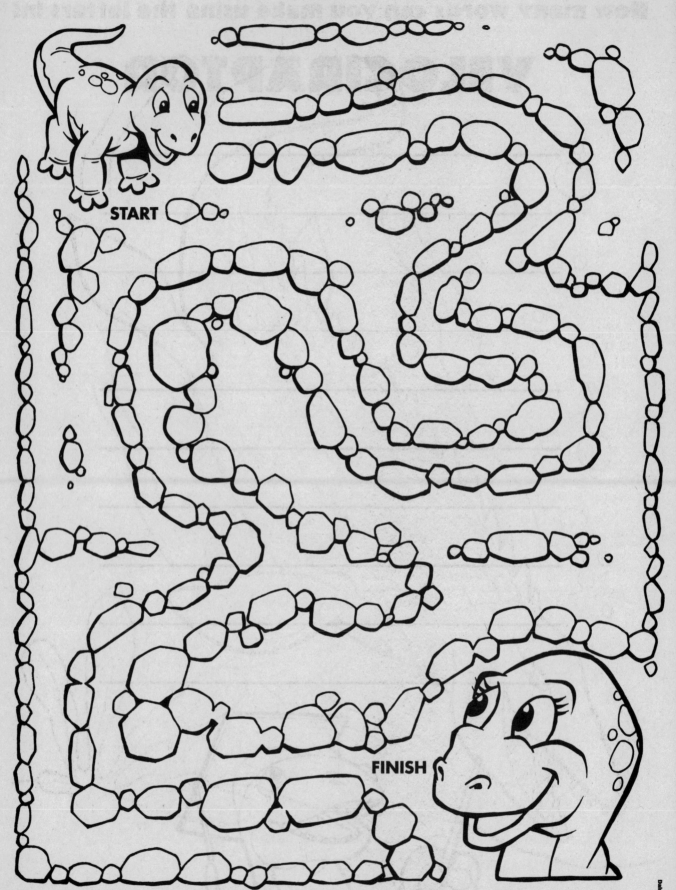

START

FINISH

USE THE GRID TO DRAW THE DINOSAUR

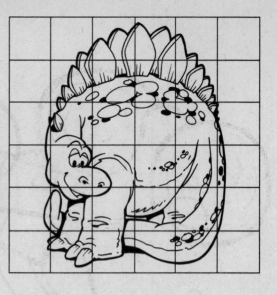

DOT-TO-DOT

How many words can you make using the letters in:

XIAOSAURUS

_____

_____

_____

_____

_____

_____

_____

_____

_____

Xiaosaurus

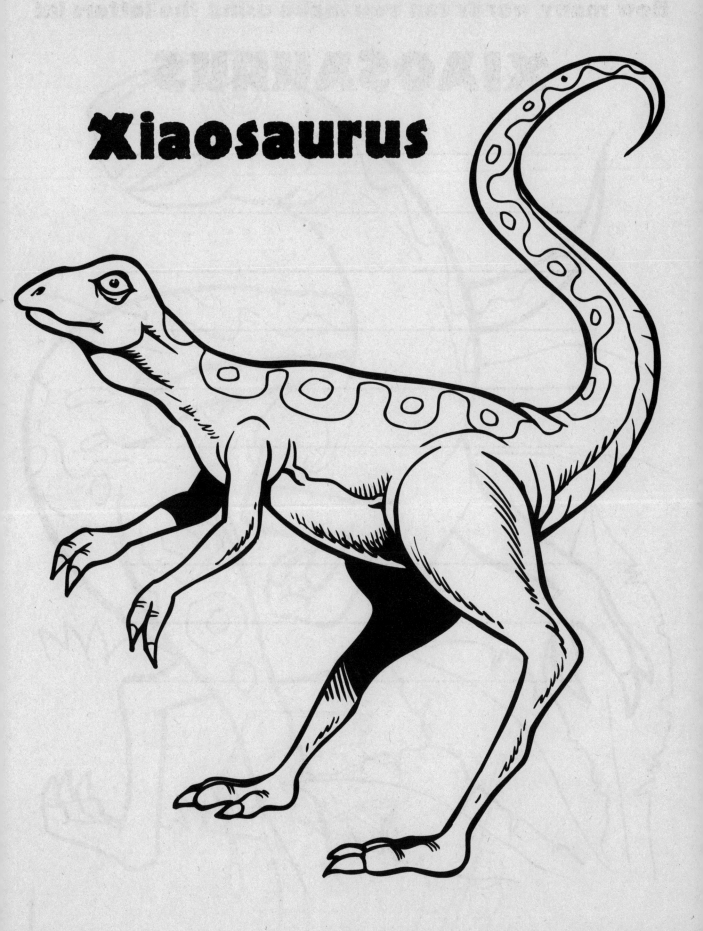

START

FINISH

SHADOW MATCHING

DOT-TO-DOT

WHICH ONE IS DIFFERENT?

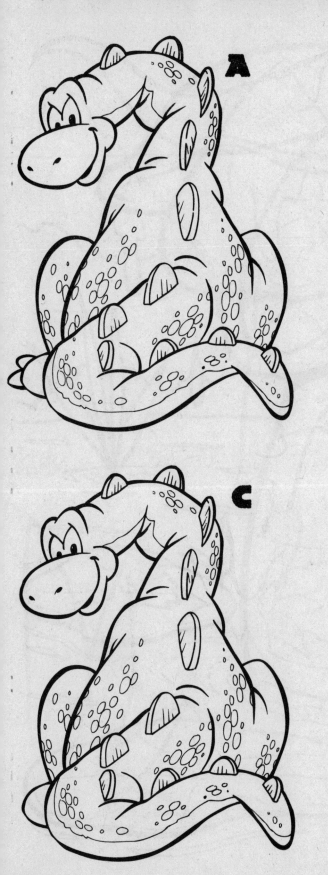

A

B

C

D

START

FINISH

USE THE GRID
TO DRAW THE
DINOSAUR

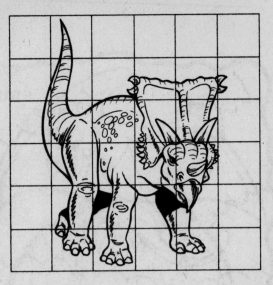

DOT-TO-DOT